Portage Public Library JUN 1 2 1991

8.95

RAINTREE SCIENCE ADVENTURES

DINOSAURS

Judith E. Greenberg and Helen H. Carey
Illustrated by Lloyd Birmingham

Raintree Publishers
Milwaukee

For Wendy — **J.G.**
For Grant — **H.C.**

Editorial
Barbara J. Behm, Project Editor
Judith Smart, Editor-in-Chief

Art/Production
Suzanne Beck, Art Director
Kathleen A. Hartnett, Designer
Carole Kramer, Designer
Andrew Rupniewski, Production Manager
Eileen Rickey, Typesetter

Reviewed for accuracy by:
Gretchen M. Alexander, Executive Director
West 40 Educational Service Center Number 5
Northlake, Illinois

Diane Gabriel
Assistant Curator of Paleontology
Milwaukee Public Museum

Copyright © 1990 Raintree Publishers Limited Partnership

All rights reserved. No portion of this book may be reproduced or utilized in any form or by any means, electronic or mechanical, including photocopying, recording, or by any information storage and retrieval system, without permission in writing from the Publisher. Inquiries should be addressed to Raintree Publishers, 310 West Wisconsin Avenue, Milwaukee, Wisconsin 53203.

Library of Congress Number: 89-78290

1 2 3 4 5 6 7 8 9   94 93 92 91 90

Library of Congress Cataloging-in-Publication Data
Greenberg, Judith E.
  Dinosaurs / by Judith E. Greenberg and Helen H. Carey;
illustrated by Lloyd Birmingham.
    (Raintree science adventures)
    Summary: Describes different kinds of dinosaurs, theories about why the dinosaurs disappeared, and the work of paleontologists.
    1. Dinosaurs—Juvenile literature. 2. Paleontology—Juvenile literature. [1. Dinosaurs.
2. Paleontology.] I. Carey, Helen H. II. Birmingham, Lloyd, ill. III. Title. IV. Series.

QE862.D5G735 1990 567.9′1   89-78290
ISBN 0-8172-3751-8 (lib. bdg.)

Before You Begin

This book takes *you* on an adventure to discover what happened to the dinosaurs! You will investigate the mystery of the dinosaurs' disappearance 65 million years ago.

You will take part in an experiment that will help explain this disappearance. You will also learn what the world was like when the dinosaurs lived and what the dinosaurs themselves were like.

Knowing the words below will help you in your adventure.

asteroid   any of the thousands of small planets in the solar system
climate   the kind of weather an area has year after year
dinosaur   a member of a group of extinct reptiles that lived on land
environment   surroundings
erupt   to burst or break out or through
extinct   no longer existing
fossil   the hardened remains or traces of a plant or an animal
marine   having to do with the sea
paleontologist   a scientist who studies fossils
preparator   a person who puts together museum displays
reptile   a cold-blooded animal with scales that breathes by means of lungs
theory   a well-researched explanation

Now turn the page, and begin your science adventure!

Digging for Dinosaurs

Today, your class went on a field trip to a **dinosaur** park. You saw the bones of the huge **reptiles** called dinosaurs that lived there millions of years ago. On the way home, you and your friend Ross decide to dig for dinosaur **fossils** next Saturday in a dry creek bed on your parents' property. Ross wants to find a bone from a type of dinosaur called the *Apatosaurus*. You want to find an *Allosaurus* bone. The *Allosaurus* had claws that could rip through the hide of its enemies.

Early Saturday morning, Ross comes to your house. Outside, you start to dig in the creek bed. You learned in school that when animals of long ago died, their bodies sometimes sank to the bottoms of creeks. The water dried up, but the fossilized bones of animals can still be found in the creek beds.

You and Ross take turns digging and sifting through the dirt. Suddenly you find something unusual.

"Wow! Look at this!" you say. "What do you think it is?"

"Maybe it's a fossil tooth!" says Ross.

"Oh, no. It's not a dinosaur's tooth at all. It's just a doll's leg. Let's go home," Ross says in a disappointed voice.

5

"Wait! Wait!" you yell. "There's something else stuck in the ground. I think it really is a dinosaur bone! Let's clean away the dirt." You brush gently around the object with a paintbrush until you can see what it is.

Ross starts jumping up and down. He shouts, "I bet it's part of a dinosaur! We found it!"

"I think you're right, Ross," you say. You put your treasure in a box and wrap your jacket around it. The two of you sit down and think about what to do next.

Ross has to go home. He promises to keep the dinosaur bone a secret. You make plans to meet each other later at the library.

You ask your mother if you can go to the dinosaur park. She says yes and drives you there. You've brought the box with the dinosaur bone along with you.

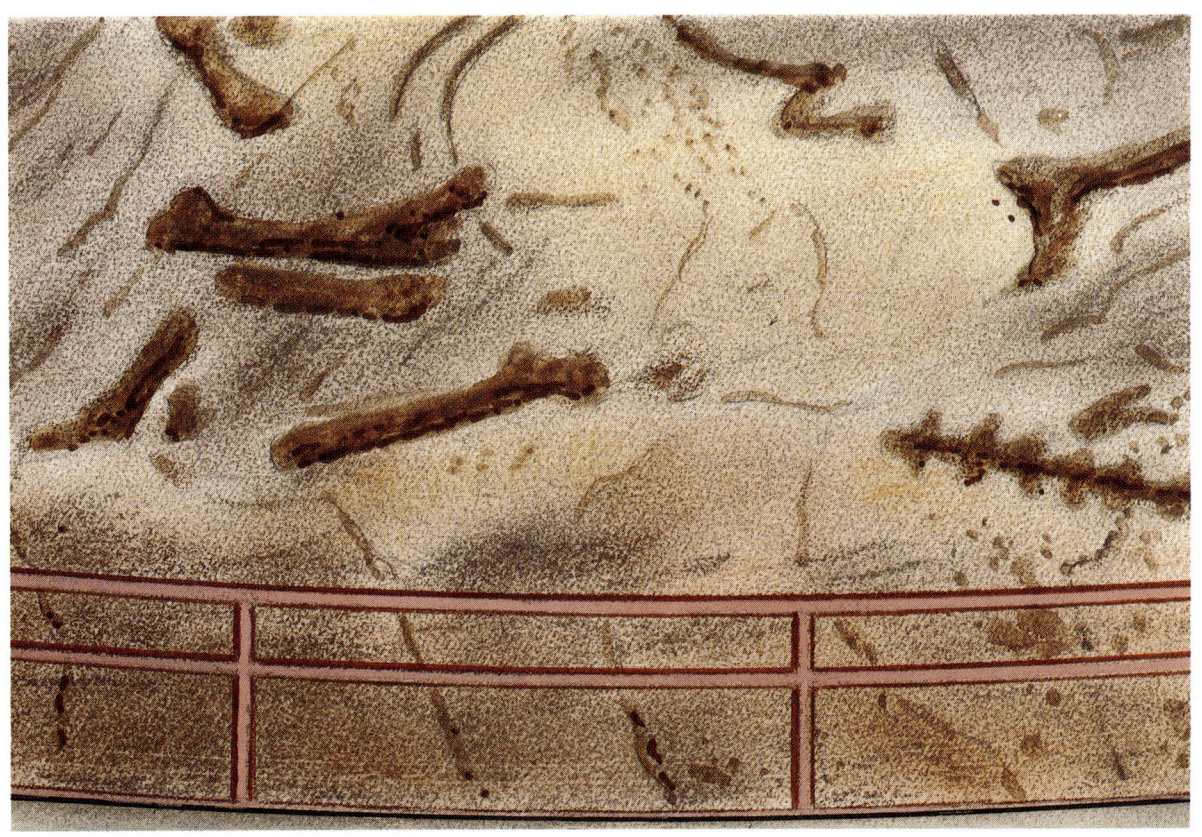

Adventure at the Dinosaur Park

At the dinosaur park, there is a cliff with over two thousand fossil bones of dinosaurs buried in the stone. You walk over to where the bones of *Brachiosaurus,* the world's largest plant-eater, are found. You put your box down and look closely at the *Brachiosaurus*'s foot. You think your discovery might be a toe or claw of this giant dinosaur. Then you remember the *Brachiosaurus* weighed as much as seven elephants. Your discovery is too small to be a *Brachiosaurus* toe or claw. You continue looking along the cliff to see if you can find a dinosaur bone that looks like your discovery.

You see the bones of dinosaurs that became **extinct** about 65 million years ago. Some dinosaurs were plant-eaters, and some ate meat. They all lived on land. You see a display of the bones of a *Tyrannosaurus rex,* the largest meat-eating land animal that ever lived. The *Tyrannosaurus rex* appears to be attacking a *Triceratops,* a plant-eater with a short horn on its nose and a long horn above each eye.

None of the bones looks like the one you found, so you keep walking and looking closely at other kinds of remains found in the rock. The bones, eggs, and leaves that you see were once parts of living animals and plants.

You tip your head way back to see the top of the cliff. You wonder how the fossils got so high up in the cliff. Then you remember what a ranger who visited your class once said. He said that this area looked very different millions of years ago. A huge, slow-moving river covered the land. What is now the cliff in front of you was part of a sandbar in the river. Movements occurred within the earth, pushing the ground up to form mountains. Because of this, fossils can sometimes be found high up in the mountains, many miles from where water is today.

Suddenly, you realize that the box you brought with you is gone.

"Oh, no! Where's my dinosaur discovery?" you gasp, as you look around frantically.

You decide to go back to the entrance of the park. That must be where you put the box down. Halfway down the cliff walkway, you stop and turn into another walkway. Halfway down this passage, you stop again. No people are around. Where is the way to the entrance? You turn into a new walkway, then into another one, and another one....

"Oh, no," you say. "I'm lost!"

You hear footsteps coming toward you.

It is dark in the walkway, and you cannot see who is coming. Out of the dark, a voice says, "Hi, there. Is this your box? Is this your jacket?"

There in front of you is a ranger. You are so glad to see him. "Oh, thanks a lot! I was beginning to get scared and a little cold."

The ranger says, "Many of the dinosaurs probably felt like you did. Scientists think that one reason dinosaurs disappeared is because their **environment** changed."

"Scientists believe that, for some reason, the **climate** got cooler. The dinosaurs didn't have fur or feathers to keep them warm," the ranger says.

"Why didn't they move to someplace warmer?" you ask.

The ranger explains, "They didn't know of anywhere else to go. Not only were the dinosaurs cold, they were hungry. The kinds of plants that they needed for food no longer grew.

"Plant-eating dinosaurs couldn't get enough to eat, and so they got weaker and died. Then the meat-eating dinosaurs, with no plant-eating dinosaurs to eat, died too."

You have many more questions, but the ranger has to leave. He points to a room down the walkway. He tells you that the ranger in that room can help you.

An Experiment

The sign on the door says:
DINOSAUR EXPERIMENTS
PLEASE COME IN

When you walk into the room, you see a ranger talking with a group of children. The ranger looks at you and says, "Welcome. We are just getting ready to talk about an experiment."

You watch the ranger put two plants of the same kind on a table. She puts a card with the phrase *grown in dark* printed on it in front of one plant. She puts a card with the phrase *grown in light* printed on it in front of the other plant. She explains that the first plant was kept in the dark for two weeks, while the second one has been in the light.

Then she asks, "What differences do you see? What do you think plants need to be healthy?"

You raise your hand. "The plant kept in the dark looks pale and sick. The plant kept in the light is strong and healthy. Plants must need light to grow well."

Holding up the weak plant, the ranger asks everyone to guess what would happen to dinosaurs who could only find unhealthy plants like this to eat, or no plants at all.

(Write your guess on a piece of paper.)

Why the Dinosaurs Died

The ranger explains that there are various **theories** about what led to the disappearance of the dinosaurs 65 million years ago.

One theory is that a large **asteroid** crashed into the earth. When this happened, billions of tons of dust blew up into the air, blocking the sun for a long time and causing darkness and freezing temperatures. Dinosaurs that survived the explosion found their world greatly changed. Plants stopped growing. Plant-eating dinosaurs starved to death. As the plant-eaters died, so did the meat-eating dinosaurs that fed off of them. Because of the cold, even more dinosaurs died.

Another theory is that **erupting** volcanoes all over the world threw out billions of tons of hot gases, rocks, and ashes high into the atmosphere. The gases and ashes floated like a cloud all the way around the earth. The cloud hung between the earth and the sun. No sunlight could get through to the earth.

Plants died without the light of the sun. All over the world, other living things died, too. Some small creatures, such as the warm-blooded animals that lived at the same time as the dinosaurs, could survive on seeds from plants. The dinosaurs, however, could not.

Another theory is that there may have been a change in the earth's climate due to movements of the continents. Scientists believe that the earth's continents once were joined in one large landmass. During the time of the dinosaurs, the landmass broke up, and the continents drifted apart. As they did so, their climates changed. It may have become too cold for the dinosaurs. Dinosaurs had trouble finding food, too, in the cooler environment. The giant ferns and grasses that plant-eating dinosaurs depended on for food did not grow well in the cold weather. Eventually, all the dinosaurs died.

The "Dinosaur Lady"

You take your fossil out of the box and hold it up to show the ranger.

She says, "It looks like a piece of a dinosaur's backbone, but I'm not sure." She tells you to talk to the "dinosaur lady" at the library.

You thank the ranger and leave the park. When you get to the library, you see Ross. You stop at a desk and ask the woman sitting there where you can find the dinosaur lady.

The woman smiles. "I'm the dinosaur lady," she says. "What do you have there?"

"We think it's a dinosaur bone. Can you tell us what it is and what dinosaur it came from?" you ask.

The librarian gently lifts the object out of the box. She examines it carefully, turning it first one way and then the other. She takes it over to the window to look at it in the sunlight.

You wonder what she is thinking. You stretch to see what she is doing. You can hardly wait for the dinosaur lady to say something.

"I'm not positive, but I think you may have found part of a backbone of a dinosaur that lived over 140 million years ago," she says.

"Do you really think it's a dinosaur bone? We were looking for dinosaur bones, but we didn't really think we'd find one," says Ross.

You wonder what your dinosaur looked like. Was it a plant-eater or a meat-eater?

The dinosaur lady suggests you visit the new dinosaur exhibit in the next room. You thank her and take your dinosaur bone with you.

The sign above the exhibit room entrance says:
> WHAT DO YOU KNOW ABOUT DINOSAURS?

Painted footprints are on the floor in front of you. You and Ross follow them into the room.

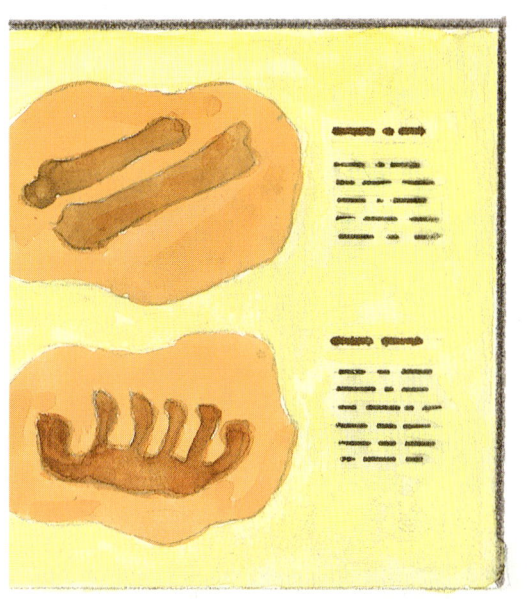

WHAT DO YOU KNOW ABOUT DINOSAURS?

How Big Were They?

Coelophysis was 8 to 10 feet (2.5 to 3 meters) long.

Plant-eaters like *Plateosaurus* had big stomachs to hold all the plants that they needed in order to live. This animal grew to 20 feet (6 m) long and walked on its hind legs.

Dinosaurs like *Stegosaurus* had thick, bony plates covering their backs. These dinosaurs were 15 to 30 feet (4.5 to 9 m) long.

Tyrannosaurus rex was the biggest meat-eating animal that ever walked the earth. It was 40 feet (12 m) long and 18 feet (5.5 m) high. The head alone of this dinosaur was as big as an average human's body.

Pteranodon's body was the size of a goose. However, the distance from the tip of one wing to the tip of the other was over 25 feet (8 m). The *Pteranodon* was not a dinosaur but a flying reptile.

Apatosaurus was 60 to 80 feet (18 to 24 m) long.

Brachiosaurus was 80 feet (24 m) long and weighed as much as seven elephants.

Diplodocus was 90 feet (27.5 m) long.

23

What Colors Were the Dinosaurs? Did They Make Sounds?

You learn many new things about dinosaurs from the exhibit. You learn that scientists do not know what colors the dinosaurs were. Their coloring was probably like that of most lizards today—green and brown. No one knows if dinosaurs had spots or stripes, or if they were one solid color.

There are other unanswered questions, too. What do you think a dinosaur sounded like? Was the sound it made like that of an elephant, a lion, or a horse? Scientists do not know. Just imagine, however, the thundering boom that a herd of *Apatosauruses* could make!

Are These Dinosaur Twins?

Some of our animals today are like dinosaurs from the past.

Triceratops

Rhinoceros

Avimimus

Roadrunner

Struthiomimus

Ostrich

25

Dinosaur Bones

When you and Ross finish studying the exhibits, you decide to visit the science museum next door. You tell the guard at the museum entrance that you may have found a dinosaur bone.

"We want to see if a scientist can tell us what kind of dinosaur bone we found," you tell the guard.

The guard takes you down a hall and knocks on a tall wooden door. A man opens the door.

"Hello," he says. "I am Dr. Harvey. I'm a **paleontologist.** I work with dinosaur fossils. May I help you?"

You show Dr. Harvey your discovery. "What kind of dinosaur do you think it's from?" you ask.

Dr. Harvey holds the fossil bone under the light on his desk. He doesn't say anything for a long time. Just when you think you can't wait another minute, he looks up. "I think you've found part of a backbone from a creature that lived in the sea," he says.

"It isn't from a dinosaur?" Ross asks.

"No, dinosaurs lived only on land. This bone is from an extinct **marine** reptile. It lived in the seas at the same time that the dinosaurs lived on land. The marine reptile whose bone you have was called a *Plesiosaur. Plesiosaurs* had long necks and paddlelike limbs," explains Dr. Harvey.

The other scientists in the room hear what Dr. Harvey is saying. They come over to look at the fossil bone. One of the paleontologists says that the bone you found could help them put together a skeleton of a *Plesiosaur*. This would help people see what one of these reptiles looked like.

"What are you going to do with your discovery?" asks Dr. Harvey. He hands the box with the bone in it back to you.

You look at Ross. He nods his head. You give the box back to the scientist. "We decided it belongs in the museum," you say. "That way, other people can see it, too."

Dr. Harvey pats both of you on the back. He says, "We're working on a new dinosaur display right now. Would you like to see what we're doing?"

"Yes!" you both shout. You follow Dr. Harvey into a workroom.

In the center of the room, people are putting dinosaur bones together to form a skeleton. Dr. Harvey explains that the skeletons are put together by people called **preparators** as well as by paleontologists. The bones are as heavy as rock. They are joined together with metal rods. Sometimes bones are missing. In that case, artificial bones are made out of plaster to fill in for the missing ones.

You look at the skeleton and wish you could have lived during the time of the dinosaurs. Then you remember that dinosaurs and people didn't live at the same time. The first dinosaurs lived more than 200 million years ago. They died out millions of years before human beings appeared.

Dr. Harvey tells you that he has a surprise for you and Ross.

Portage Public Library

Dr. Harvey gives your box back to you. He asks you to look inside. It's your fossil bone! How is that possible? You gave it to the museum. Why is he giving it back?

Dr. Harvey smiles. "It's not the real bone. While you and Ross were looking at the dinosaur skeleton, the museum sculptors quickly made a plaster cast of your discovery for you to keep. Do you like it?"

"It looks just like the real bone!" you say.

You and Ross are thrilled to have the treasure. You both decide that you will work very hard in school so that you can study dinosaurs when you grow up.

What kind of science adventure would you like to go on next?

31814850137941

PORTAGE PUBLIC LIB   00423

J567.9   JUN 1 2 1991   Por.
G
    Greenberg, Judith E
      Dinosaurs

Portage Public Library